AWESOME DOGS

Cocker Spaniels

by Nathan Sommer

BELLWETHER MEDIA • MINNEAPOLIS, MN

Note to Librarians, Teachers, and Parents:

Blastoff! Readers are carefully developed by literacy experts and combine standards-based content with developmentally appropriate text.

Level 1 provides the most support through repetition of high-frequency words, light text, predictable sentence patterns, and strong visual support.

Level 2 offers early readers a bit more challenge through varied simple sentences, increased text load, and less repetition of high-frequency words.

Level 3 advances early-fluent readers toward fluency through increased text and concept load, less reliance on visuals, longer sentences, and more literary language.

Level 4 builds reading stamina by providing more text per page, increased use of punctuation, greater variation in sentence patterns, and increasingly challenging vocabulary.

Level 5 encourages children to move from "learning to read" to "reading to learn" by providing even more text, varied writing styles, and less familiar topics.

Whichever book is right for your reader, Blastoff! Readers are the perfect books to build confidence and encourage a love of reading that will last a lifetime!

This edition first published in 2018 by Bellwether Media, Inc.

No part of this publication may be reproduced in whole or in part without written permission of the publisher. For information regarding permission, write to Bellwether Media, Inc., Attention: Permissions Department, 5357 Penn Avenue South, Minneapolis, MN 55419.

Library of Congress Cataloging-in-Publication Data

Names: Sommer, Nathan, author.
Title: Cocker Spaniels / by Nathan Sommer.
Description: Minneapolis, MN : Bellwether Media, Inc., [2018] | Series: Blastoff! Readers: Awesome Dogs | Audience: Age 5-8. | Audience: K to grade 3. | Includes bibliographical references and index.
Identifiers: LCCN 2016052718 (print) | LCCN 2017005258 (ebook) | ISBN 9781626176119 (hardcover : alk. paper) | ISBN 9781681033419 (ebook)
Subjects: LCSH: Cocker spaniels—Juvenile literature.
Classification: LCC SF429.C55 S66 2018 (print) | LCC SF429.C55 (ebook) | DDC 636.752/4—dc23
LC record available at https://lccn.loc.gov/2016052718

Editor: Betsy Rathburn   Designer: Kathy Petelinsek

Printed in the United States of America, North Mankato, MN.

Table of Contents

What Are Cocker Spaniels?

Cocker spaniels are happy dogs with long ears. They are gentle **companions** who love to play.

People call them cockers for short.

Cockers are strong and **sturdy**. They have medium-sized bodies.

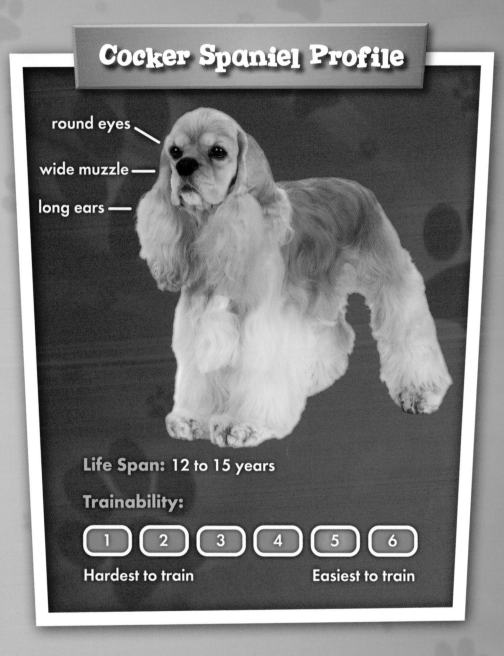

Cocker Spaniel Profile

round eyes

wide muzzle

long ears

Life Span: 12 to 15 years

Trainability:

1 2 3 4 5 6

Hardest to train

Easiest to train

They can weigh up to
30 pounds (14 kilograms).

7

Flowing Coats and Round Eyes

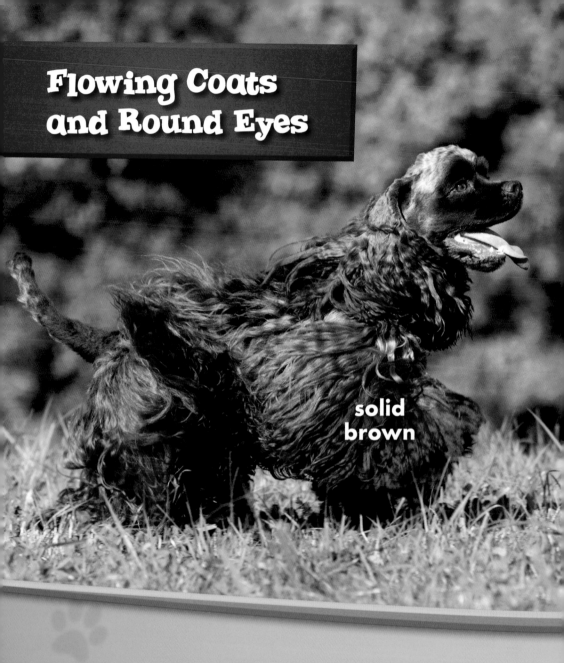

solid
brown

Cockers have flowing,
medium-length **coats**. Their
hair can be straight or wavy.

8

Cocker Spaniel Coats

parti-color
black

parti-color
red

solid
black

Coats can be **solid** or **parti-color**. Black, brown, and red are common colors.

muzzle

Cockers have rounded heads. Their faces have wide **muzzles** and square jaws.

These dogs have round, dark eyes.

History of Cocker Spaniels

Cockers are in the spaniel family of dogs. Many people believe spaniels began in Spain.

Spain

N
W · E
S

The spaniel family has been
around for hundreds of years.

Cockers were first **bred** to be hunting dogs. They came to the United States during the 1870s.

Americans soon fell in love with this smart **breed**!

The **American Kennel Club** added cocker spaniels in 1878. They are the smallest members of the **Sporting Group**.

Cockers are still popular today!

Easygoing Dogs

Cockers have a lot of energy. They like to play fetch and go on long walks.

These active pets love to chase birds and small animals.

agility event

Cockers are **intelligent**, too. They can learn tricks and compete in **agility** events.

After playtime, they love
to cuddle!

Glossary

agility—a dog sport where dogs run through a series of obstacles

American Kennel Club—an organization that keeps track of dog breeds in the United States

bred—purposely mated two dogs to make puppies with certain qualities

breed—a type of dog

coats—the hair or fur covering some animals

companions—friends who keep someone company

intelligent—able to learn and be trained

muzzles—the noses and mouths of some animals

parti-color—a pattern that is mainly one color, but with patches of one or more other colors

solid—one color

Sporting Group—a group of dog breeds that are active and need regular exercise

sturdy—strongly built

To Learn More

AT THE LIBRARY
Gray, Susan H. *Cocker Spaniels*. New York, N.Y.:
AV2 by Weigl, 2017.

Landau, Elaine. *Cocker Spaniels Are the Best!*
Minneapolis, Minn.: Lerner Publications, 2011.

Mathea, Heidi. *Cocker Spaniels*. Edina, Minn.:
ABDO Pub. Co., 2011.

ON THE WEB
Learning more about
cocker spaniels is as
easy as 1, 2, 3.

1. Go to www.factsurfer.com.

2. Enter "cocker spaniels" into the search box.

3. Click the "Surf" button and you will see a
   list of related web sites.

With factsurfer.com, finding more information
is just a click away.

Index

The images in this book are reproduced through the courtesy of: Eric Isselee, front cover; Lenkadan, pp. 4-5; steamroller_blues, p. 5; Eudyptula, pp. 6, 9; WilleeCole Photography, p. 7; Vera Zinkova, pp. 8-9; beronb, pp. 10-11; Volodymyr Burdiak, p. 11; otsphoto, pp. 12, 19; GROSSEMY VANESSA/ Alamy, p. 13; Ksenia Raykova, pp. 14-15; Mostovyi Sergii Igorevich, pp. 15, 21; Olga Kuzyk, p. 16; PaylessImages, p. 17; OliverJW, p. 18; Mark Herreid, p. 20.

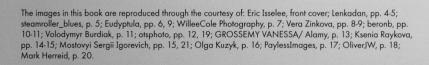